Multi Color Hope Bracelet
by Suzanne Balistreri
Make these bracelets to honor a cause close to your heart. This assurance of hope is a perfect gift for someone special in your life.

Hope charm
Swarovski crystals
6mm bicone
Silver 3mm balls

SIZE: 7½"
BASIC SUPPLIES: Crimp pliers • Wire cutter

MATERIALS:
18 *Swarovski* crystals assorted 6mm bicone
1 Sterling Hope charm
22 Sterling 3mm balls
1 Silver toggle clasp
2 Sterling 2mm crimp beads
9" of beading wire .014 or .015

INSTRUCTIONS:
Attach the toggle to the wire with a crimp bead. Hide the wire tail inside the first 2 beads. String a ball and a crystal for a total of 9 times. Next, string 2 balls, a charm, 1 ball. Repeat the pattern for a total of 9 times. Add a crimp bead. Run the wire through the toggle and back around through the crimp bead, ball and 1 crystal. Crimp. Trim wire tail as needed.

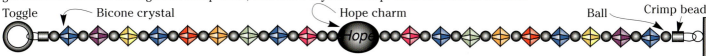

Pink Ribbon Awareness Bracelet
Make or wear a glittering expression of hope and care.

SIZE: 7½"
BASIC SUPPLIES
Crimp pliers • Wire cutter

MATERIALS:
9 *Swarovski* crystals Rose 8mm round faceted
20 *Swarovski* crystals Clear 4mm bicone
10 *Swarovski* crystals Rose 4mm round faceted
2 Sterling 3mm balls
1 breast cancer charm
1 Silver heart toggle clasp
2 Sterling 2mm crimp beads
9" of beading wire .014 or .015

INSTRUCTIONS:
Attach a toggle to the wire with a crimp bead. Hide the wire tail inside a 3mm ball and 2 beads. String: bicone, Rose 4mm ball, bicone, Rose 8mm ball. Repeat for a total of 9 times. End with the charm, bicone, Rose 4mm ball, bicone, and 3mm ball. Add a crimp bead. Run wire through the toggle and back around through the crimp bead, ball and 1 crystal. Crimp. Trim wire tails as needed.

Awareness Colors

 Pink — Breast Cancer

 Light Purple — Epilepsy or Lupus

 Green — Organ Donation or Kidney Cancer

 Gold — Childhood Cancer

 Red — Aids or Women's Heart Disease

 Light Blue — Prostate Cancer

 Yellow — Amber Alert or Support your Troops

 Purple — Alzheimer's Disease

 Teal — Ovarian Cancer

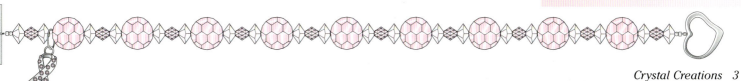

Coin Pearl Jewelry Set

Pearls come in all shapes, sizes and colors. Coin pearls are a favorite because each one is just a bit different from the next, but oh, so pretty.

In this project you will learn how to use chain, double wire wrap head pins and use seed beads as an accent to create you own one of a kind piece.

Fancy Sterling chain with rings

9 mm Coin pearls

Swarovski crystals Lt. Rose Satin AB 5mm bicone

TOHO 3-cut trans-lustered seed beads

SIZE: Necklace 15"-17", Bracelet 7½", Earrings 1½"

TIP: You will only use 137 *TOHO* beads but sometimes they get crushed accidentally when wire wrapping. Always buy extra.

BASIC SUPPLIES:
PLIERS - Crimp • Round-nose • Split Ring • Flat-nose • Wire cutter

Necklace
MATERIALS:
14½" fancy Sterling chain with rings to attach wrapped head pins
44 Sterling Silver 2" head pins
14 coin pearls 9mm
30 *Swarovski* crystals Lt Rose Satin 5mm AB bicone
144 *TOHO* 3-cut 15/0 trans-lustered seed beads
2" of Sterling medium chain for necklace extender
2 Sterling split rings
Silver lobster claw

INSTRUCTIONS:
Thread all beads on head pins before wire working. See Wrapped Loop instructions on page 7. Hang 13 coin pearl head pins in the center with 14 crystal head pins on each side. Attach a clasp to each end with a split ring. Add 2 crystals and coin pearl to end of extender chain to give it a finished touch.

Earrings

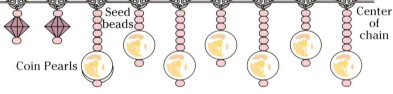

MATERIALS:
2 pieces 1" long fancy Sterling chain with rings to attach wrapped head pins
2 coin pearls 9mm
14 *TOHO* 3-cut 15/0 trans-lustered seed beads
2 Silver 2" head pins
1 pair of ear wires

INSTRUCTIONS:
Thread beads onto a head pin. See Wire Wrapping on page 7. Open the bottom loop of the ear wire with Flat-nose pliers and slide onto the end of the chain. Close the loop.

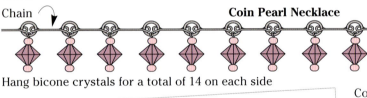

Coin Pearl Necklace

Hang bicone crystals for a total of 14 on each side

Seed beads — Coin Pearls — Center of chain

Bracelet
MATERIALS:
8 coin pearls 9mm
54-60 *TOHO* 3-cut 15/0 trans-lustered seed beads (you will need 54 to make a 7½" bracelet)
9 *Swarovski* crystals Lt Rose Satin 5mm AB bicone
2 Silver 2mm balls or larger beads used next to each crimp
1 Sterling Silver clasp
2 Sterling Silver 2mm crimp beads
9" of beading wire .014 or .015

INSTRUCTIONS:
Attach a clasp to the wire with a crimp bead. Crimp. Hide the wire tail inside the first few beads. Start with Silver 2mm all or larger bead and follow the stringing diagram until all the beads are used. End with a crimp bead.

Thread wire through the crimp bead and a few beads of the bracelet. Crimp. Trim excess wire. Before crimping, make sure that the wire you have pulled through beads is not too tight. Trim wire tails as needed.

Bracelet

Crystal Creations 5

Timeless Crystals

Jet Black crystals have a special sparkle and depth of color. They make every ensemble richer. Make a beautiful bracelet or earrings, or replace an old watchband with beautiful crystals.

 Bali Silver daisy spacer beads

 Swarovski crystals
Jet Black 6mm donut
Jet Black 5mm bicone
Jet Black 4mm bicone

 Silver Watch face, holes running 12 to 6

SIZE: 7½"

BASIC SUPPLIES
PLIERS - Crimp • Round-nose • Flat-nose • Wire cutter

Watch

MATERIALS:
1 watch face with holes running 12 to 6
12 *Swarovski* crystals Jet Black 6mm donut
2 *Swarovski* crystals Jet Black 5mm bicone
2 *Swarovski* crystals Jet Black 4mm bicone
12 fancy Bali spacers
2 Bali silver spacer discs
1 flat daisy Bali spacer
1 small Silver toggle
2 Silver 2mm crimp beads
2 pieces of beading wire .014 or .015, each 7" long

INSTRUCTIONS:
Loop 1 wire through one side of the watch hole bringing both ends together and string a Bali disc. Follow the stringing diagram over both pieces of wire. String: crystal donut and fancy spacer for a total of six times. When you have come to the end of your pattern, put on a 5mm bicone crystal and crimp bead. Run both pieces of wire through the toggle and back through the crimp bead and bicone. Crimp. Trim wire tail as needed. Repeat for the second half of the watch. To embellish the clasp: On a head pin, thread a 4mm bicone, flat daisy Bali spacer and a 4mm bicone. Wire Wrap it, see page 7.

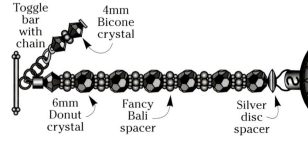

Basic Wire Wrapping

Wrapping for projects in this book can all be done with Round-nose pliers and small wire cutters.

TIP: If this is your first time wire wrapping, use a small Silver or Gold ball at the very top of the head pin for added protection so you do not accidentally snap off your top bead.

Wrapped Loop:
(1) Thread beads onto a 2" head pin.

(2) Turn a loop at the top by grasping pin with Round-nose pliers about 1/8" from end of pliers. Gently touch the top bead. Bend head pin at a 90° angle. Loosen your grip on the pliers and pivot them from horizontal to vertical. Apply pressure to pliers again when your work looks like the next diagram.

(3) Wrap wire over the top jaw of pliers. Reposition the wire on the bottom jaw of pliers and wrap the wire around it to form a loop.

(4) Hold the loop in place with pliers and coil the short end of wire around the neck.

Begin coils as close to the loop as possible. Make 2-3 coils, then clip the end of wire close to the coils.

Using Round-nose pliers, tuck in any little remnant of wire.

Dangles: Open loop on ear wires. Thread dangle into the loop. Close ear wire loops.

Chain: If you are wire wrapping and attaching head pins to a chain, first slide chain onto loop before you finish and make the final close of head pin.

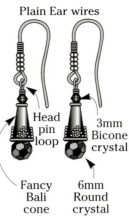

Plain Ear wires

Head pin loop
Fancy Bali cone
3mm Bicone crystal
6mm Round crystal

Earrings
Size: 1"
MATERIALS:
2 Silver 2" head pins
2 small Bali cones
2 *Swarovski* crystals Jet Black 6mm round faceted
2 *Swarovski* crystals Jet Black 3mm bicone
2 Fishhook *Bali* ear wires

INSTRUCTIONS:
On a head pin, thread a round crystal, Bali cone and bicone crystal. Wire wrap head pin. See Wrapped Loop on this page. Use Flat-nose pliers to open an ear wire, slip on head pin loop and close ear wire.

Bali Silver cone
Swarovski crystals, Jet Black 6mm round

Bracelet
SIZE: 7½"
MATERIALS:
19 Silver 2" head pins
39 *Swarovski* crystals faceted Jet Black 6mm round
40 flat daisy *Bali* spacers
9" of beading wire .014 or .015
2 Silver 2mm crimps
1 Silver toggle clasp

INSTRUCTIONS:
Wire Wrap 19 round crystals on 2" head pins. See Wire Wrapping on this page. Thread 1 crimp and spacer on end of wire. String: crystal, spacer, head pin and spacer. Repeat for a total of 19 times. Thread spacer and crimp bead. Run wire through the toggle back through the crimp bead, spacer and crystal. Crimp. Repeat for the other side of bracelet. Trim as needed.

Bali spacer beads

Swarovski crystals Jet Black 6mm round

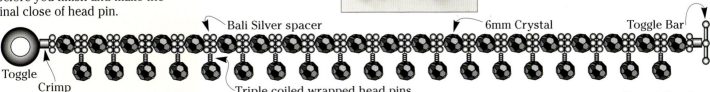

Toggle — Crimp — Bali Silver spacer — Triple coiled wrapped head pins — 6mm Crystal — Toggle Bar

Sparkles Necklace

Crystals
Seed beads
Trim tail
Fancy crimps

Sparkles Necklace
by Gail Wing

Sometimes a simple crystal necklace is all it takes to complete your outfit. This necklace doubles as a five stranded wrist wrap bracelet.

Swarovski crystals 4mm bicone

SIZE: 39"

BASIC SUPPLIES:
Crimp pliers
Wire cutter

MATERIALS:
39 each *Swarovski* crystals 4mm (Amethyst, Light Amethyst, Black Diamond, Rose Satin)
1 gram *TOHO* 11/0 #21F Silver seed beads
1 gram *TOHO* 11/0 metallic cut seed beads
2 Silver 2mm crimp beads
1 mini alligator clip
40" of beading wire .014 or .015

INSTRUCTIONS:
Sort crystals into 4 piles and seed beads into 2 piles. Begin by attaching the mini alligator clip on one end of the wire. String 2 crimp beads. Follow the stringing diagram at left. When you finish the pattern, remove the alligator clip and thread the end of the wire through both crimp beads and seed beads. Gently pull ends in opposite directions to tighten it up. Crimp. Trim wire tails as needed.

Multi Crystal Glitz Bracelet

Encircle your wrist with a rainbow of glitzy sparkle.

Swarovski crystals 4mm bicone

Bali 2-strand spacer beads

SIZE: 7½"
BASIC SUPPLIES: Crimp pliers • Wire cutter

MATERIALS:
82 *Swarovski* crystals assorted 4mm bicone
9 Bali 2-strand spacer beads
2 pieces of .014 or .015 beading wire 10" long
12 Sterling Silver 2mm balls
1 Silver toggle
2 Silver 2mm crimp beads

INSTRUCTIONS:
Use 1 wire to work each side of the bracelet. Thread a crimp bead, bicone, 3 balls, spacer bead. String 5 different color crystals, 1 spacer. Repeat for a total of 8 groups. Thread 3 balls, a bicone and a crimp bead. Tape wire ends to hold the beads in place or use a mini alligator clip until you are ready to crimp. Repeat for the second strand. When you come to the end, run the second strand into the last bicone and crimp bead. Take both ends and bring them through the toggle and back up through the crimp bead and bicone. Crimp. Trim wire tails as needed.
Follow the same steps for the toggle bar.

Toggle — Crimp — Balls — Bicone crystals — Bali spacer

Necklace

MATERIALS:
52 Peachy 5mm freshwater pearls
78 *Swarovski* crystals Violet Opal 4mm champ
2 grams *TOHO* size 15 Silver lined seed beads
1 flower 1" pendant
2" Sterling Silver chain
25 small Bali fancy spacers
2 Sterling 3mm balls
1 Silver lobster claw clasp
1 Silver split ring
2 Sterling 2mm crimp beads
51 Silver 2" head pins
24" of beading wire .014 or .015

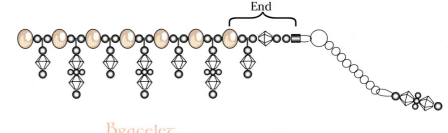

INSTRUCTIONS:
Thread all beads on head pins before doing any wire wrapping.

Short dangle: Make 26.
String: seed bead, crystal, seed bead.

Long dangle: Make 25.
String: seed bead, crystal, Bali spacer, crystal, seed bead. See Wire Wrapping instructions on page 7. For this project you will fully close the loops. Attach 1 long fringe to the end of the chain.

Pendant: Cut 6" of wire for a 3-strand bail. Run wire from the back of the hole in the pendent to the front leaving a ½" tail or less. Thread a few seed beads and a crimp bead onto the back wire. Secure the loose end with a mini alligator clip or tape while you are forming the bails of the pendent.

Thread seed beads onto the other side of the wire forming your first loop of the bail. Bring the wire to the back of the pendent and pass it through the hole. Thread seed beads to form the second bail, again bringing it from front to back. Thread seed beads to form the third bail but when you bring it to the back, take it through the crimp bead, pulling it tight. Crimp. Trim wire tails as needed.

3-Strand seed bead Bail

Pendant

For the bracelet repeat pattern for a total of 9 times

Necklace: Cover the center of 18" of wire with 12 seed beads. Slide the pendent to the middle of the wire over the beads.

String from the middle to the end. String: pearl, seed bead, short dangle, seed bead, pearl, seed bead, long dangle and seed bead.

Repeat this pattern for a total of 12 times.

End the first side of the necklace by adding a pearl, seed bead, short dangle, seed bead, pearl, 2 seed beads, crystal, seed bead, ball and crimp bead. Thread wire through clasp and back around through the crimp bead and ball. Crimp. Trim wire tail as needed.

Repeat bead pattern for the other side of the necklace.

Finish: Add a pearl, seed bead, short dangle, seed bead, pearl, 2 seed beads, crystal, seed bead, ball, crimp bead. Pass the wire through a split ring and back through the crimp bead. Crimp. Trim wire tails as needed. Add chain to split ring.

Bracelet

MATERIALS
22 Peach 5mm pearls
35 *Swarovski* crystals Violet Opal 4mm champ
1 gram *TOHO* size 15 Silver lined seed beads
1½" Sterling Silver chain
11 small Bali fancy spacers
2 Sterling 3mm balls
1 Silver lobster claw clasp
1 Silver split ring
2 Sterling 2mm crimp beads
22 Silver 2" head pins
9" of beading wire .014 or .015

INSTRUCTIONS:
Fringe: See instructions for Necklace.
Make 11 of each kind of head pin. Attach 1 long head pin to the end of the chain.

Bracelet: On 9" of wire, thread a crimp bead, ball, seed bead, crystal, seed bead. Follow the stringing pattern given in the necklace for a total of 10 times.

End the bracelet by threading on a seed bead, pearl, seed bead, short dangle, seed bead, pearl, seed bead, crystal, seed bead, ball and crimp bead.

Next thread wire through a split ring and back through the crimp bead and ball. Crimp. Trim wire tail as needed.

Use Split Ring pliers to add the chain.

Chandelier Earrings

MATERIALS:
1 pair of fancy chandelier earrings
6 Silver 2" head pins
2 Peach 5mm pearls
12 *Swarovski* crystals Violet Opal 4mm champ
26 *TOHO* seed beads size 15, Silver lined
6 small Bali fancy spacers

INSTRUCTIONS:
For each earring make 2 outer dangles. Thread a seed bead, crystal, seed bead, Bali spacer, seed bead, crystal and seed bead on head pin.

For center dangle, thread a seed bead, pearl, seed bead, crystal, seed bead, Bali spacer, seed bead, crystal and seed bead.

See Wire Wrapping instructions on page 7.
Attach dangles to each chandelier earring.

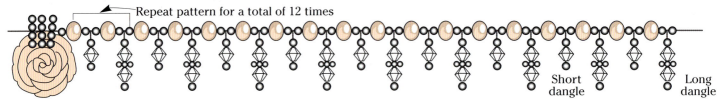

Repeat pattern for a total of 12 times

Short dangle

Long dangle

Pretty Woman

Even on rainy days, peachy pearls, crystals and chandelier earrings will always make a woman feel pretty.

Swarovski crystals
Violet Opal 4mm champ
Silver 3mm balls
Bali fancy spacers
Silver lined seed beads - size 15
Peach 5mm pearls

SIZE: Necklace 15", Bracelet 7½", Earrings 2"

BASIC SUPPLIES: PLIERS - Crimp • Round-nose • Split Ring • Wire cutter

Elegant Affair
by Penny Craig

Bright light splashes from silver and pink crystal. Dress up your favorite silk blouse or give that little black dress some extra sparkle with this Elegant Affair.

SIZE: Necklace 16", Bracelet 8", Earrings ¾"

BASIC SUPPLIES:
PLIERS - Crimp • Round-nose • Flat-nose • Split Ring • Wire cutter

Swarovski crystals
    Rose 6mm AB
    Rose 4mm AB
    Rose 8mm AB 2X
    Clear 4.5mm AB rondelles
    Clear 4mm transmissions

Diamond crowned
    8mm rondelles

TOHO Aiko seed beads
    White
    Matte Rose

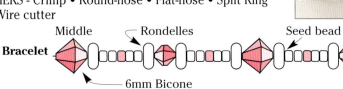
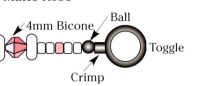

Necklace

MATERIALS:
- 1 gram *TOHO* Aiko TB-21F White seed beads
- 1 gram *TOHO* Aiko TB-563F Matte Rose seed beads
- 8 *Swarovski* crystals Rose 8mm AB 2X bicone
- 6 *Swarovski* crystals Rose 6mm round
- 6 *Swarovski* crystals Lt Rose 4mm bicone
- 4 Diamond crowned 8mm rondelles
- 3 *Swarovski* crystals Clear 4mm transmissions
- 8 *Swarovski* crystals 4.5mm AB rondelles
- 2 Sterling 2mm crimp beads
- 1 Silver lobster claw clasp
- 1 Sterling split ring
- 18" of beading wire .014 or .015

INSTRUCTIONS:
This is the pattern from the middle to one end, begin at the middle.
String: Clear crystal, Rose crystal, rondelle, large crystal, crowned rondelle, large crystal, rondelle, Rose crystal, Clear crystal, Rose crystal, rondelle, large crystal, crowned rondelle, large crystal and rondelle. Next string on 4 White seed beads, 1 Rose seed bead, 4 White seed beads, 1 Rose seed bead, 4 White seed beads, 1 Rose seed bead, 4 White seed beads, 1 Rose seed bead, 4 White seed beads, 1 Rose seed bead, 1 round crystal. Repeat for a total of 3 times. End with 1 Rose seed bead, 4 White seed beads, 1 Rose seed bead, 4 White seed beads, 1 Rose seed bead. Run wire through the clasp and back through crimp bead and ball. Crimp. Trim excess wire. Start at the beginning, repeat for other side.

Bracelet

MATERIALS:
- 48 *TOHO* Aiko TB-21F White seed beads
- 12 *TOHO* Aiko TB-563F Matte Rose seed beads
- 5 *Swarovski* crystals Rose 8mm AB 2X
- 6 *Swarovski* crystals Rose 6mm AB
- 22 *Swarovski* crystals 4.5mm AB rondelles
- 2 Sterling 2mm balls
- 2 Sterling 2mm crimp beads
- 1 Silver lobster claw clasp
- 1 Sterling split ring
- 10" of beading wire .014 or .015

INSTRUCTIONS:
This is the pattern from the middle to one end, beginning at the middle. String: large crystal, rondelle, 2 White seed beads, Rose seed bead, 2 White seed beads, rondelle, small crystal, rondelle, 2 White seed beads, Rose seed bead, 2 White seed beads, rondelle. Repeat the pattern twice. End the row by stringing on 2 White seed beads, Rose seed bead, 2 White seed beads, a ball and a crimp bead. Thread wire through the clasp and back through the crimp bead and ball. Crimp. Trim wire tail as needed. Starting at the beginning, repeat for the other side.

Earrings

MATERIALS:
- 2 *Swarovski* crystals Rose 6mm AB
- 2 *Swarovski* crystals Rose 4mm AB
- 6 White size 11 matte seed beads
- 2 Silver 2" head pins
- 2 Silver ear wires

INSTRUCTIONS:
On a head pin, thread a White seed bead, large crystal, White seed bead, small crystal and White seed bead. Wire wrap head pin. See steps 1-5 on page 7. Use Flat-nose pliers to open your ear wire, slip on head pin loop and close ear wire.

Crystal & Ribbon Necklaces

These quick and easy necklaces are lovely for weddings, proms and just going out around town.

This is one of the pendants made from *Swarovski* Bezel Set Button Component.

SIZE: 16"
BASIC SUPPLIES: 2 pair Flat-nose pliers

MATERIALS:
- 1 *Swarovski* Bezel Set Button Component (small, medium or large)
- 1 Sterling jump ring (5mm for small pendant, 6mm for large pendent)
- 16" finished 13mm wide ribbon or 2mm super fine cording

INSTRUCTIONS:
Attach jump ring to pendant. Thread the ribbon through the jump ring.

Necklace

MATERIALS:
14" Sterling chain with built in loops
2" Silver medium chain to use as an extender
1-2 grams *TOHO* size 11 Silver lined seed beads
14 *Swarovski* crystals Black Diamond 8mm faceted helix
    (1 crystal is used for the chain extender)
26 *Swarovski* crystals Black Diamond 6mm bicone
1 Silver lobster claw clasp
2 Sterling split rings
40 Sterling 2" head pins
    (1 head pin is used for the chain extender)

INSTRUCTIONS:
Thread all of your beads on head pins before wire working. See Wire Wrapping on page 7. Do not close head pins until attached to the circle of chain. See step 5 on page 7. Find the center of the chain and hang an 8mm crystal dangles. Hang six 8mm crystal dangles on each side. Next add 13 bicone crystal dangles on each side. Attach split ring and extender chain onto the last open ring of chain. On a head pin, thread a seed bead, 8mm crystal and 3 seed beads. Wire work head pin and attach to end of extender chain. Attach clasp with a split ring.

Bracelet

MATERIALS:
1 gram *TOHO* size 11 Silver lined seed beads
2 size 8 Silver lined seed beads
15 *Swarovski* crystals Black Diamond 6mm
9" of beading wire .014 or .015
2 Sterling 2mm crimp beads
1 Sterling clasp
1 Silver split ring

INSTRUCTIONS
Attach clasp to 1 end of the wire with a crimp bead. String: 1 size 8 seed bead. Begin pattern with 5 size 11 seed beads, 1 crystal. Repeat the pattern for a total of 15 times. Finish by threading on 5 size 11 seed beads, a size 8 seed bead and a crimp bead. Thread wire through the clasp, bringing it back through the crimp bead and the seed bead. Crimp. Trim wire tail as needed.

Earrings

MATERIALS:
2 *Swarovski* crystals Black Diamond 8mm faceted helix
2½" of chain
2 Sterling 2" head pins
2 Sterling euro ear wires
8 *TOHO* size 11 Silver lined seed beads

INSTRUCTIONS
Thread pattern onto a 2" head pin. Start with seed bead, 8mm crystal, 3 seed beads. See page 7 for wire wrapping instructions. Remember not to finish wire wrapping the head pin until you slide the head pin onto the bottom loop of chain. Use Flat-nose pliers to open your ear wire, slip on top chain, and close ear wire.

Black Diamond Trio

Surround your neck with delicate dangles of crystal fringe.

Silver lined seed beads size 11

Swarovski crystals
Black Diamond
6mm bicone
8mm faceted helix

Earrings

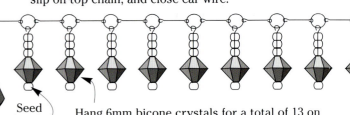

SIZE: Necklace 14"-16", Bracelet 7"

BASIC SUPPLIES:
PLIERS: Crimp • Flat-nose • Round-nose
• Split Ring • Wire cutter

Necklace
Starting from center of chain hang six 8mm faceted helix crystal dangles to the right and six to the left for a total of 13.

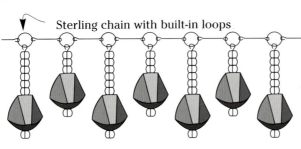

Sterling chain with built-in loops

Seed beads

Hang 6mm bicone crystals for a total of 13 on each side.

Bracelet

Crystal Creations 15

Always a Bridesmaid

Wonderful for a wedding or special occasion, pearls and crystals are a perfect match.

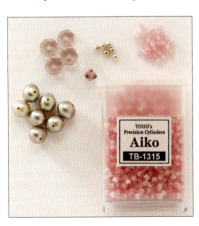

Light Sea Foam Green 6mm pearls

Swarovski crystals Rose 4mm bicone

Czech glass Lt. Rose 6mm roundels

Sterling Silver balls 2mm

TOHO Aiko Pink cylinder beads

SIZE: Necklace 16½", Bracelet 7½", Earrings 3¾"

BASIC SUPPLIES:
PLIERS - Crimp • Round-nose • Split Ring • Wire cutter

Earrings

MATERIALS:
2 Silver 2" head pins
1 Pair of 3" ear threads with a bottom loop
4 Sterling Silver 2mm balls
2 *Swarovski* crystals Rose 4mm bicone
2 *TOHO* Aiko Pink size 11 cylinder beads
2 Czech glass Lt. Rose 6mm roundels

INSTRUCTIONS:
On a head pin, thread beads following the beading diagram. Start with cylinder bead, roundel, ball, bicone and ball. See Wire Wrapping on page 7.

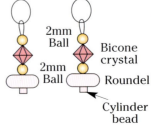

Chain extender with crystal dangles for the tip of the necklace and bracelet.

Bracelet

Crystal Creations 15

Always a Bridesmaid

Wonderful for a wedding or special occasion, pearls and crystals are a perfect match.

Light Sea Foam Green 6mm pearls

Swarovski crystals Rose 4mm bicone

Czech glass Lt. Rose 6mm roundels

Sterling Silver balls 2mm

TOHO Aiko Pink cylinder beads

SIZE: Necklace 16½", Bracelet 7½", Earrings 3¾"

BASIC SUPPLIES:
PLIERS - Crimp • Round-nose • Split Ring • Wire cutter

Earrings

MATERIALS:
2 Silver 2" head pins
1 Pair of 3" ear threads with a bottom loop
4 Sterling Silver 2mm balls
2 *Swarovski* crystals Rose 4mm bicone
2 *TOHO* Aiko Pink size 11 cylinder beads
2 Czech glass Lt. Rose 6mm roundels

INSTRUCTIONS:
On a head pin, thread beads following the beading diagram. Start with cylinder bead, roundel, ball, bicone and ball. See Wire Wrapping on page 7.

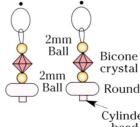

Chain extender with crystal dangles for the tip of the necklace and bracelet.

Bracelet

MATERIALS:
- 7 Light Sea Foam Green 6mm pearls
- 1 gram of *TOHO* Aiko #1315 cylinder beads or Pink size 11 round beads
- 13 *Swarovski* crystals Rose 4mm bicone
- 7 Czech Light Rose glass roundels
- 2 Sterling Silver 2mm crimp beads
- 27 Sterling Silver 2mm balls
- 2 Sterling Silver 3mm balls
- 1 Silver split ring
- 1 Silver lobster claw clasp
- 2" Sterling Silver chain
- 9" of beading wire .014 or .015

INSTRUCTIONS:
Attach clasp to one end of the wire with a crimp bead. Hide the wire tail inside a Silver 3mm ball. String: 2mm ball, bead, pearl, bead, ball, bicone, ball, roundel, ball and bicone for a total of 7 times. End pattern with 3mm ball and crimp bead. Thread the wire through a split ring taking it back through the crimp bead and ball. Crimp. Trim wire tail as needed. Attach chain to the split ring. On the first head pin, thread a bead, roundel and ball. On the second head pin, thread on bead, bicone and bead. Wire wrap head pin. See Wire Wrapping on page 7. Attach the loops to the chain. Close the loop.

Necklace

MATERIALS:
- 16 Light Sea Foam Green 6mm pearls
- 3 grams of *TOHO* Aiko #1315 cylinder beads or Pink size 11 round beads
- 33 *Swarovski* crystals Rose 4mm bicone
- 16 Czech glass Lt Rose 6mm roundels
- 2 Sterling Silver 2mm crimp beads
- 66 Sterling Silver 2mm balls
- 2 Sterling Silver 3mm balls
- 1 Silver split ring
- 1 Silver lobster claw clasp
- 2" Sterling Silver chain
- 18" of beading wire .014 or .015

INSTRUCTIONS:
Follow the instructions for the bracelet, repeating the stringing pattern for a total of 16 times.

Flower Power Bracelet

Remember the flower chains you braided when you were a child? These bluebells capture those memories with a sparkle that never fades. The Flower bracelet is a fun way to dress up a pair of jeans.

Swarovski Flower slider
Swarovski crystals Clear 4mm bicone
Seed beads size 11 Black

SIZE: 7½"

BASIC SUPPLIES:
PLIERS - Crimp • Split ring • Wire cutter

MATERIALS:
- 5 *Swarovski* flower sliders
- 6 *Swarovski* crystals Clear 4mm bicone AB
- 1 gram size 11 Iridescent Blue seed beads
- 2 Sterling 3mm balls
- 2 Sterling 2mm crimp beads
- 1 Silver lobster claw clasp
- 1 Silver split ring
- 2 pieces of beading wire .014 or .015, each 9" long

Sample 1 View from back   View from top

INSTRUCTIONS:
Thread both ends of the wire through the clasp and secure with a crimp bead. Slide a 3mm ball over both wires and hide the thread tails inside. Separate wires. On each wire, thread 5 seed beads. Pass both wires through a bicone. Separate the wires.
Stringing Pattern: On each wire, string 5 seed beads, a flower, and 5 seed beads. Pass both wires through a bicone. Repeat this pattern for all flowers. End by separating the wires and stringing 5 seed beads on each wire. Pass both wires through a 3mm ball, a crimp bead, and split ring. Return the wires through the crimp bead and hide the tails inside the ball. Crimp. Trim wire tail as needed.

Crimp — Ball — AB Clear crystal — Flower slider — Seed beads

Cosmo Girl Earrings

SIZE: Earrings 3¾"

BASIC SUPPLIES:
Round-nose pliers • Wire cutter

MATERIALS:
5mm *Swarovski* crystals
 (4 Jet Black, 2 Clear)
Two 3" earring threads

INSTRUCTIONS:
On each ear thread, string a Silver ball, Black crystal, Clear crystal, and Black crystal.

Black & White Polka Dot Bracelet

Polka dot lampwork beads bring lighthearted fun to your accessory wardrobe.

Swarovski crystals
Clear 5mm
Black 4mm

Lampwork beads
11mm

SIZE: 8"

BASIC SUPPLIES:
PLIERS - Crimp • Split Ring • 2 pair Flat-nose • Wire cutter

MATERIALS FOR BRACELET:
5 Lampwork 11mm beads
6 Bali 5mm beads
2 Sterling 2mm balls
14 *Swarovski* crystals Black 4mm bicone
12 *Swarovski* crystals Clear 5mm faceted spacers
Silver medium size toggle clasp
2 Sterling 2mm crimp beads
1 Silver jump ring
1 Silver split ring
10" of beading wire .014 or .015

Bracelet
INSTRUCTIONS:
Begin: Attach a jump ring and a split ring to the circle end of the toggle. Thread a crimp bead, ball and Black crystal onto the wire. Attach toggle by passing the wire through the split ring and back through the crimp bead, ball, and crystal. Crimp. Trim wire tail as needed.

String: Clear crystal, Black crystal, Bali spacer, Black crystal, Clear crystal and lampwork bead. Repeat the pattern 5 times. Next, string a Clear crystal, Black crystal, Bali spacer, Black crystal, Clear crystal, Black crystal. Finish by threading on a 2mm ball and crimp bead. Next run your wire through the toggle and back through the crimp bead, ball and Black crystal. Crimp. Trim wire tail as needed.

Bracelet

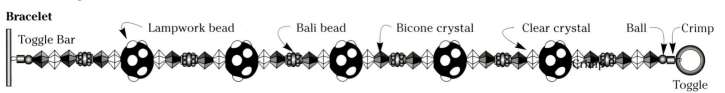